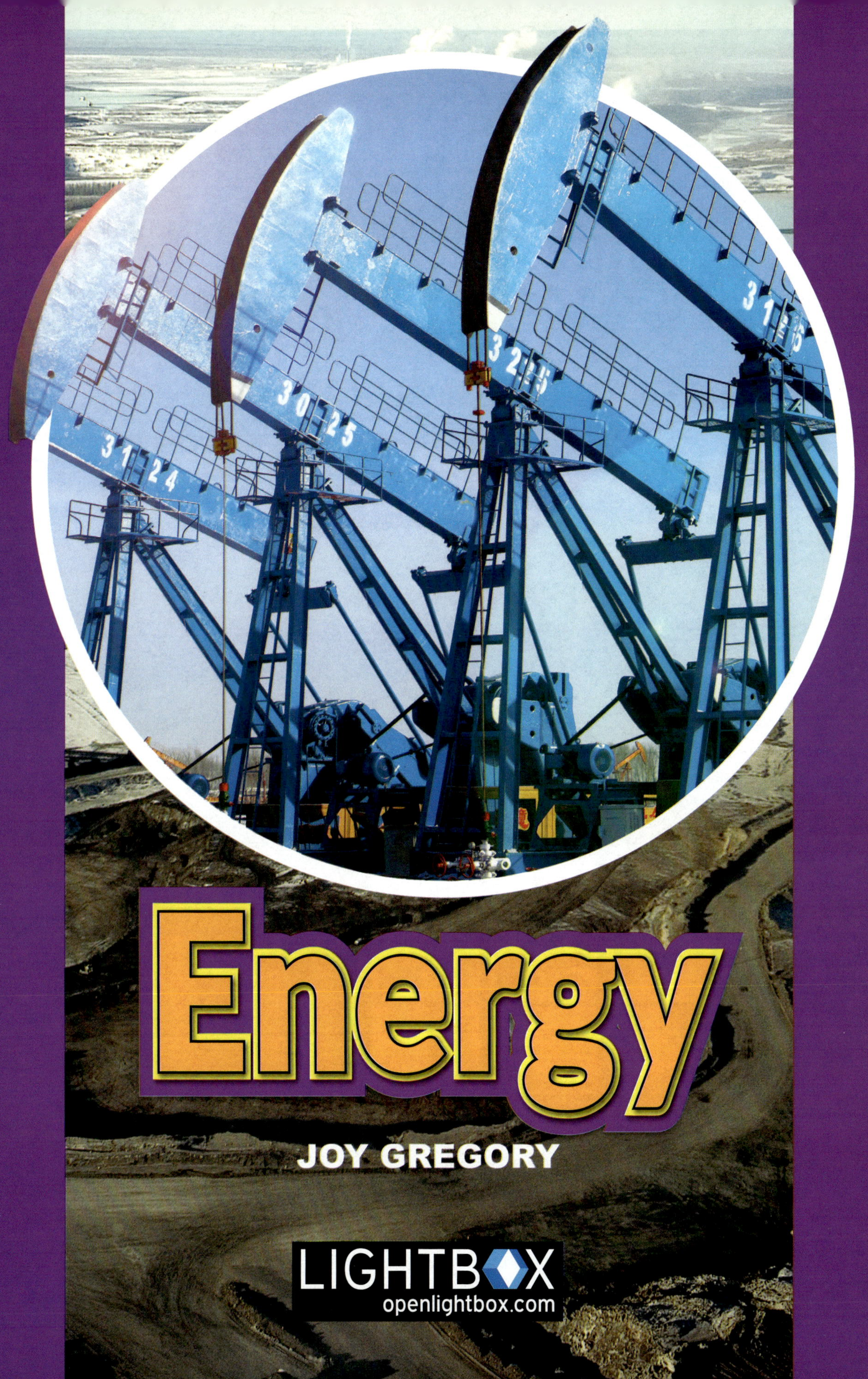
Energy
JOY GREGORY
LIGHTBOX
openlightbox.com

Lightbox is an all-inclusive digital solution for the teaching and learning of curriculum topics in an original, groundbreaking way. Lightbox is based on National Curriculum Standards.

STANDARD FEATURES OF LIGHTBOX

AUDIO High-quality narration using text-to-speech system

ACTIVITIES Printable PDFs that can be emailed and graded

SLIDESHOWS Pictorial overviews of key concepts

VIDEOS Embedded high-definition video clips

WEBLINKS Curated links to external, child-safe resources

TRANSPARENCIES Step-by-step layering of maps, diagrams, charts, and timelines

INTERACTIVE MAPS Interactive maps and aerial satellite imagery

QUIZZES Ten multiple choice questions that are automatically graded and emailed for teacher assessment

KEY WORDS Matching key concepts to their definitions

CONTENTS

Energy in the United States

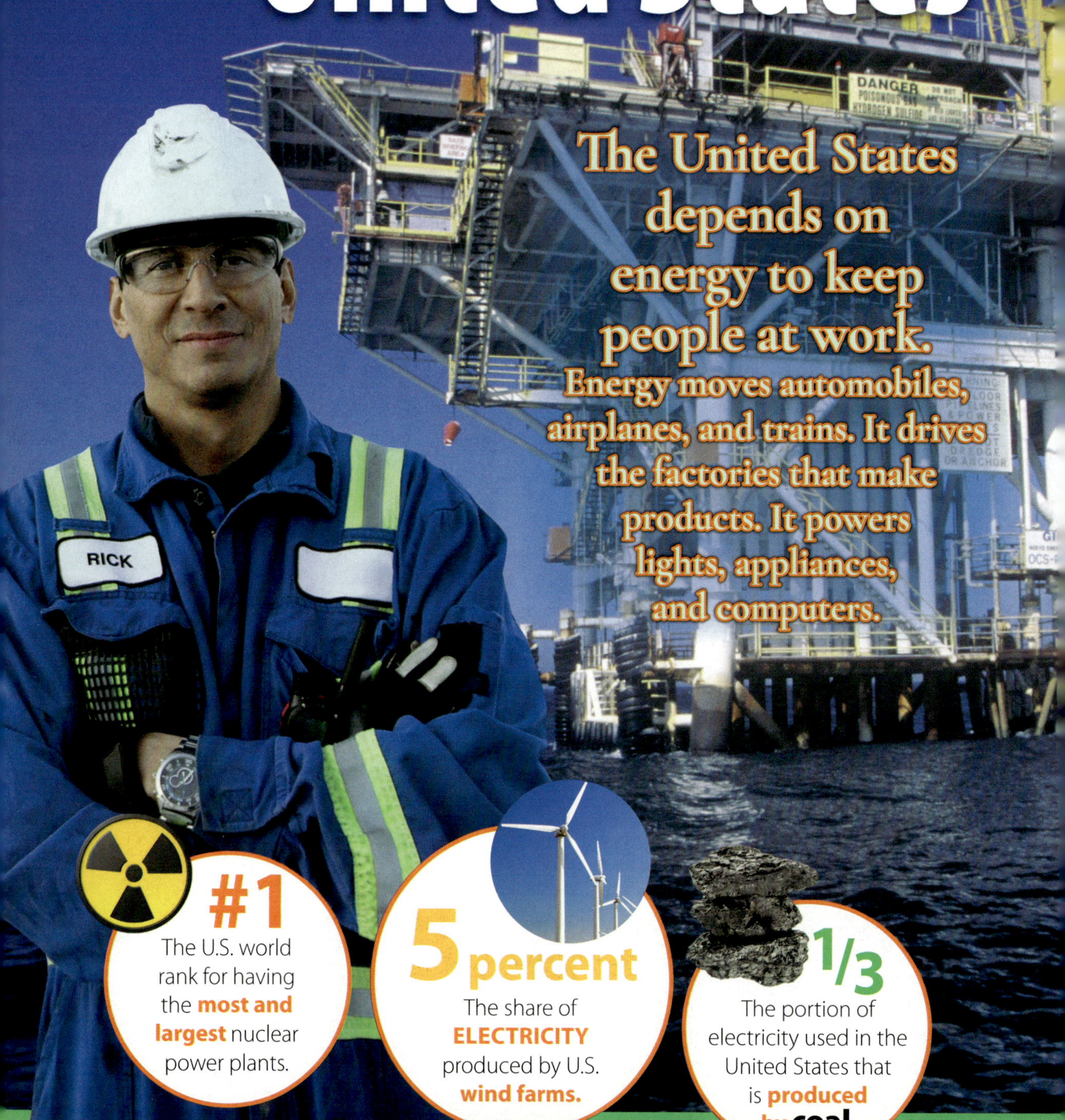

The United States depends on energy to keep people at work. Energy moves automobiles, airplanes, and trains. It drives the factories that make products. It powers lights, appliances, and computers.

#1
The U.S. world rank for having the **most and largest** nuclear power plants.

5 percent
The share of **ELECTRICITY** produced by U.S. **wind farms.**

1/3
The portion of electricity used in the United States that is **produced by coal**.

The United States is a world leader in the **production** of energy. More than 80 percent of the energy produced in the United States comes from **fossil fuels**. These are natural gas, oil, and coal. The United States is also a world leader in energy **consumption**. Per capita, people in the United States use more than four times the energy consumed by the rest of the world.

The energy created by burning fossil fuels is nonrenewable. Once this type of energy is used, it is gone. Nuclear energy, made from the mineral uranium, is considered nonrenewable. This is because uranium deposits are **finite**.

Renewable sources of energy are **regenerated** by nature. These include energy created by the wind, Sun, and water. The energy produced by water is called hydroelectricity or hydropower. Another source of renewable energy is biomass. Biomass comes from plants and includes wood, which can be burned to make heat or electricity. Geothermal energy is generated by the natural heat inside Earth. It is another renewable source of energy.

Energy Then and Now

Energy use in the United States has changed over time. Some of these changes came with the development of new ways to generate energy. Other changes are related to the different uses of energy.

Getting Around

Early Americans traveled on foot or by wagon. By the 1800s, steam-powered boats were used for river transport. Today, airplanes, trains, and motor vehicles move people and goods to work and school.

THEN

NOW

Heating the Home

During the 1900s, most Americans began to heat their homes with gas or oil rather than coal. Today, about 60 percent of U.S. homes burn natural gas. About 100 million U.S. homes are air conditioned.

THEN

NOW

Less than 1 percent of motor vehicles in the United States are powered by electricity, but the proportion is growing.

Power in the Home

In the 1800s, lamps burned gas or kerosene, but electricity was introduced to homes by the 1930s. Today, electricity powers everything from lights to appliances and computers.

THEN

NOW

Working with Machines

In the past, U.S. factories were powered by water wheels or by coal-fired electrical plants. Today, most U.S. factories run on electricity generated by natural gas, coal, and nuclear energy.

THEN

NOW

Energy Resources in the United States

Every state produces at least some of the energy it needs. That energy is generated from different sources. For example, every state produces at least some wind and solar energy. Solar energy is powered by the Sun.

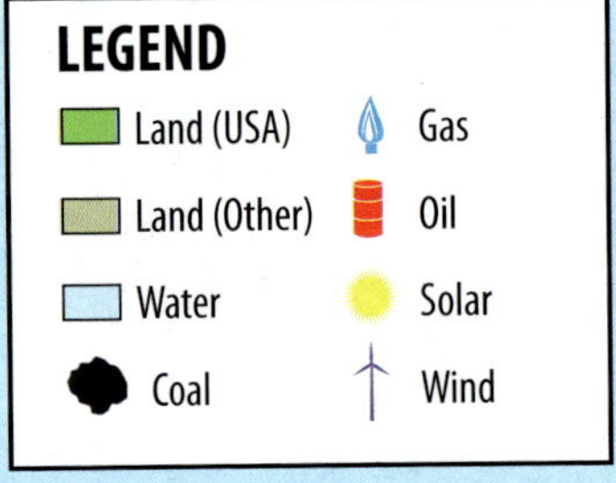

SCALE 400 MILES 700 KILOMETERS

Pacific Ocean

1 SOLAR POWER
California

Located in Rosamond, California, the Solar Star power station is one of the world's largest solar farms. There are other large solar farms in California, Arizona, and Nevada.

2 COAL MINE
Wyoming

Wyoming is home to the North Antelope Rochelle Mine, the largest coal mine in the world. The other top coal-mining states in the U.S. are West Virginia, Kentucky, Illinois, and Pennsylvannia.

3 WIND FARM Oregon

Shepherds Flat Wind Farm near Arlington in eastern Oregon makes enough renewable energy to power 235,000 homes. Other states known for their wind farms are Texas, Iowa, and California.

4 OIL & GAS Texas

Port Arthur Refinery in Texas is the largest oil refinery in the United States. Texas, North Dakota, Alaska, California, and New Mexico are the most oil-rich states in the country.

Energy Products Ranked by Importance

Individuals and businesses in the United States generate about $18 trillion in goods and services every year. The total of these goods and services is called the **gross domestic product (GDP)**. Less than 4 percent of the U.S. GDP comes from energy. The GDP linked to energy is divided into four sectors. These sectors are utilities, oil and gas extraction, petroleum and coal products, and pipeline transportation.

Coal is mined in 38 states. Most coal comes from Wyoming, West Virginia, Kentucky, Pennsylvania, and Montana.

Utilities are companies that provide heating, fuel, and power to people. Utilities generate about 1.6 percent of the GDP. The process of extracting oil and gas from beneath the ground or the ocean generates about 1.1 percent.

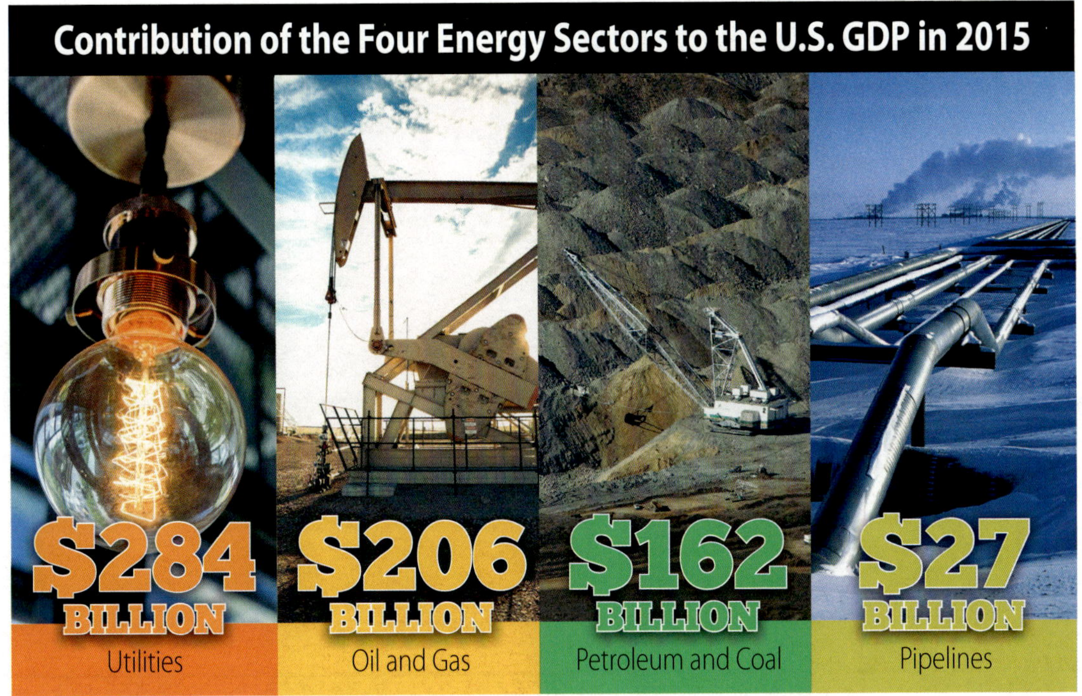

The GDP from oil and gas extraction rose in the early 2000s. This was the result of **horizontal drilling** and **hydraulic fracturing**. These processes increased production of oil and gas found in **shale** deposits.

Petroleum and coal contribute about 0.9 percent to the U.S. GDP. Petroleum products are made from **refining** crude oil and natural gas into other products. These products include gasoline, diesel, and airplane fuel. Above-ground and underground pipelines are used to transport natural gas and crude oil from where they are found to refineries. Pipelines represent about 0.1 percent of the total GDP.

There are around 30 offshore rigs in the Gulf of Mexico. The rigs are built in harbors, then towed out to sea and partly sunk into position. They drill for oil and natural gas.

Timeline of Energy Events

During the 1800s, cities in the United States started using coal-fired electricity to run factories, and to light streets and buildings. The automobile was invented in 1886. Its popularity helped oil become the country's most important source of energy by the 1950s.

1850	1860	1870	1880	1900

1859. Edwin Drake successfully drills for oil in Titusville, Pennsylvania.

1878-82. Thomas Edison invents a light bulb that lasts 40 hours. Four years later, he opens the first coal-powered electricity station in New York City and supplies electricity to homes.

1941. Grand Coulee Dam on the Columbia River begins operating. It is the biggest hydroelectric dam in the country.

1957. A nuclear power plant at Santa Susana, California opens. It is the first nuclear plant to sell electrical power in the United States.

1984. Nuclear power plants replace hydropower as the largest source of electricity in the United States next to coal and natural gas.

1950 | 1970 | 1990 | 2000 | THE FUTURE

1973. The University of Delaware builds its first solar energy collectors.

2015. 64 percent of the new power plants opened in 2015 use renewable sources to generate electricity.

U.S. Energy in the World

The United States is the world's largest producer of natural gas. It is the second-largest producer of coal and the third-biggest producer of crude oil. The United States produces about 91 percent of the energy it consumes. The rest of its energy needs are met by **importing** energy from other countries.

Steady winds blow across some areas of the United States, making them ideal locations for wind farms.

Most of the energy imported to the United States comes as petroleum. This comes in the form of natural gas, crude oil, or refined petroleum products. In 2015, the United States imported more than 9 million barrels per day of petroleum. Nearly 80 percent of those imports were in the form of crude oil.

The majority of the crude oil shipped to the United States comes from five countries. Canada is the country's largest supplier of crude oil. The rest of the crude oil comes from Saudi Arabia, Venezuela, Mexico, and Colombia.

2ND PLACE

The U.S. ranks behind China as the **WORLD'S LARGEST** producer and consumer of electricity.

#20

The U.S. position on the list of countries that produce **ELECTRICITY** from **nuclear fuel.**

20 MILLION

barrels of petroleum products are consumed in the United States each day.

Coal is the largest energy **export** from the United States. It is the only form of U.S. energy with more exports than imports. The Netherlands is the biggest buyer. This country sells U.S. coal to other countries in Europe. The United States also exports some petroleum. Canada and Mexico are the two largest buyers. These two countries also buy electricity from the United States.

Coal is so heavy that the easiest way to transport it is by river. Tugs pull or push long barges of coal joined together in rows.

Facing the Issues

Critics say the energy business harms the environment. Pollution is one problem. Burning fossil fuels releases **toxic** substances into the air. Rain washes the air pollution into lakes, rivers, and oceans.

When coal and petroleum products are burned to create energy, they release carbon dioxide into the atmosphere. Carbon dioxide is a greenhouse gas. It traps heat from the Sun. Scientists say carbon dioxide is the biggest cause of climate change.

Oil and gas spills harm wildlife. Other wildlife deaths are related to renewable energy. Birds and bats are killed by the rotating blades of wind **turbines**.

Solar farms radiate a lot of heat. Animals and birds can be burned if they get too close to the solar panels.

Debate

Critics claim that above-ground pipelines damage the environment. They are also potential sources of pollution through leaking. Some people object that pipelines cross areas of wilderness or regions that have spiritual meaning to Native Americans. Should people build more pipelines?

YES

- Pipelines are the least expensive way to ship oil and gas products
- The service is reliable because the flow of product in pipelines is not affected by factors such as weather or traffic
- When pipelines are buried, the land above them can be used to grow food or for roads

NO

- Long pipelines are difficult to maintain and monitor for holes that cause leaks
- Leaky pipelines harm the environment by releasing oil or gas that poisons plants and animals
- Pipelines disturb unspoiled areas of wilderness and the animals that live there

Biomass includes waste products of other industries, such as wood dust created by forestry and lumber operations.

Looking to the Future

The United States is a world leader in the production of green energy. Green energy is energy made from renewable resources. It reduces carbon dioxide emissions and other toxic pollutants released by burning petroleum products and coal.

About 13 percent of U.S. electrical power is generated from renewable sources. About 6 percent of that comes from hydropower. Another 7 percent comes from other renewables, including 5 percent from wind. Biomass, solar, and geothermal sources generate less than 3 percent of electricity produced in the United States, but their use is growing. Scientists are also working to harness other renewable forms of energy, including ocean tides.

The United States has some of the world's largest reserves of fossil fuels. Reserves are resources that have not yet been extracted. Scientists are looking for ways to make this energy greener by capturing the carbon dioxide created when these fuels burn.

Power plants using biomass are concentrated in the northwest, the Great Lakes region, and in states along the eastern seaboard.

Careers in Energy

Energy employs millions of U.S. workers. A career in energy is a good choice for people who like teamwork, running machines, and solving problems. Some people work outdoors mining raw resources such as coal and oil. Others drive trucks or build the electrical lines and pipelines that deliver energy to consumers. A growing number of workers help turn renewable and nonrenewable energy into electricity and fuel.

Petroleum Engineer
Petroleum engineers design ways to extract oil and gas from Earth. They work with scientists who study rock formations that hold oil and gas. They tell oil rig workers how and where to place the drills that extract fossil fuels from underground.

Duties: Managing the daily operations of drilling rigs

Education: A bachelor's degree in petroleum engineering

Interests: Math, science, machines, and rock formations

Wind Turbine Technician
Wind turbine technicians make sure the engines that turn wind energy into electricity keep working. Some work in factories that make turbines. Others have to travel to where wind farms are located.

Duties: Making, installing, maintaining, and repairing wind turbines

Education: Technical college training in engine repair, plus on-the-job-training

Interests: Outdoor work, machinery repair, and no fear of heights

Power Line Installers
Power line installers install and repair electrical power systems in **urban** and **rural** areas. They climb power poles or work with machines that lift them to power lines high above the ground.

Duties: Install and repair high-voltage electrical wires

Education: Apprenticeship training

Interests: Outdoor work, attention to detail, and no fear of heights

Activity

Create climate change in a jar. You will need these items:

- 2 Empty jars
- 6 Ice cubes
- Plastic wrap
- Brightly-lit window
- Timer
- Pencil and paper to record findings

Instructions

1. Clean the jars. Let them air dry and come to room temperature.
2. Place the jars side-by-side in a brightly lit window or under a desk lamp.
3. Put three ice cubes in each jar.
4. Cover the top of the first jar with plastic wrap.
5. Leave the second jar open.
6. Record observations every five minutes for 30 minutes.
7. What did you observe? While the open jar remains clear as the ice melts, did the covered jar mist up with droplets of water?

What happened?

The plastic wrap acts like Earth's atmosphere and traps heat from the Sun or light inside the jar. The heat also causes condensation, in the form of water that builds up on the inside of the jar. This is the equivalent of how heat trapped in the atmosphere changes the climate on Earth.

Quiz

Check out how much you have learned about energy in the United States. The answers to all these questions are in this book.

ONE
In what is the United States a world leader?

TWO
Where is the world's largest solar power plant located?

THREE
What are two species of animal harmed by wind farms?

FOUR
What is the job title of someone who designs ways to extract oil and gas?

FIVE
How much more energy do Americans consume compared with people in the rest of the world?

SIX
Why is carbon dioxide called a greenhouse gas?

SEVEN
In what year did the Grand Coulee Dam open?

NINE
From what country does the U.S. import most of its crude oil?

TEN
What share of crude oil in the United States is transported by pipelines?

EIGHT
What is the name of the type of energy created from heat beneath Earth's surface?

ANSWERS
ONE The production and consumption of energy
TWO Rosamond, California **THREE** Birds and bats
FOUR Petroleum engineer **FIVE** Four times as much
SIX It traps heat in Earth's atmosphere **SEVEN** 1941
EIGHT Geothermal **NINE** Canada **TEN** 70 percent

Key Words

consumption: process of consuming or using a product

export: to sell products to another country

finite: has limits or a definite end

fossil fuels: fuels formed underground by dead plants and animals

gross domestic product (GDP): the total value of the goods and services a country or area produces

horizontal drilling: a way to reach oil and gas deposits in the ground, in which a drill moves horizontally rather than straight down from the well

hydraulic fracturing: the process of pumping water, sand, and chemicals into the ground to force out gas from shale rock

importing: the process of bringing goods into a country

production: the creation of goods

refining: in energy, the process of turning a natural resource into another product

regenerated: made again

rural: relating to the countryside

shale: a porous type of rock that traps fossil fuels

toxic: poisonous

turbines: rotary engines moved by wind

urban: relating to a city

Index

LIGHTBOX

SUPPLEMENTARY RESOURCES

Click on the plus icon found in the bottom left corner of each spread to open additional teacher resources.

- Download and print the book's quizzes and activities
- Access curriculum correlations
- Explore additional web applications that enhance the Lightbox experience

LIGHTBOX DIGITAL TITLES

Packed full of integrated media

VIDEOS

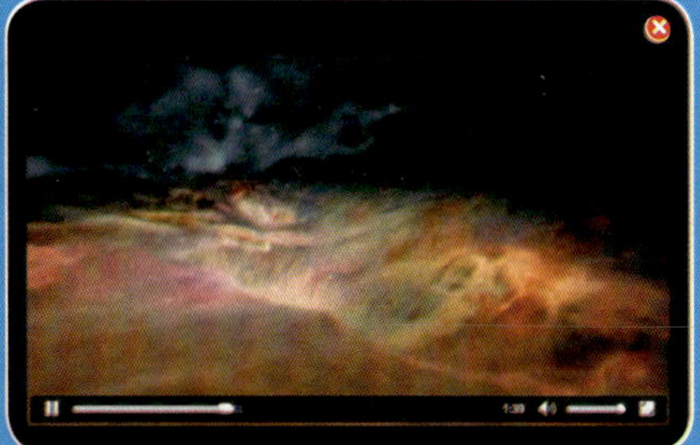

INTERACTIVE MAPS

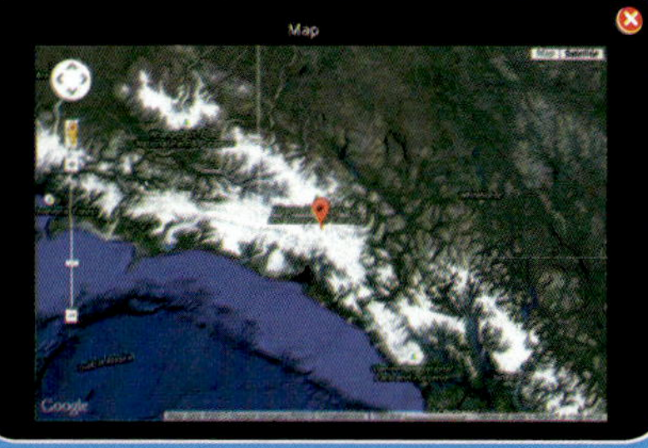

WEBLINKS

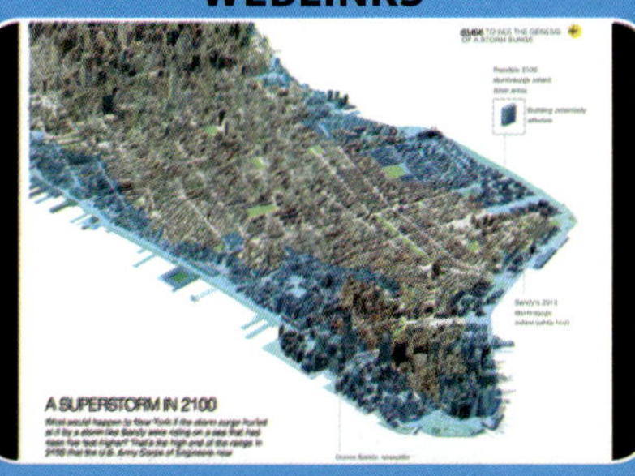

SLIDESHOWS

QUIZZES

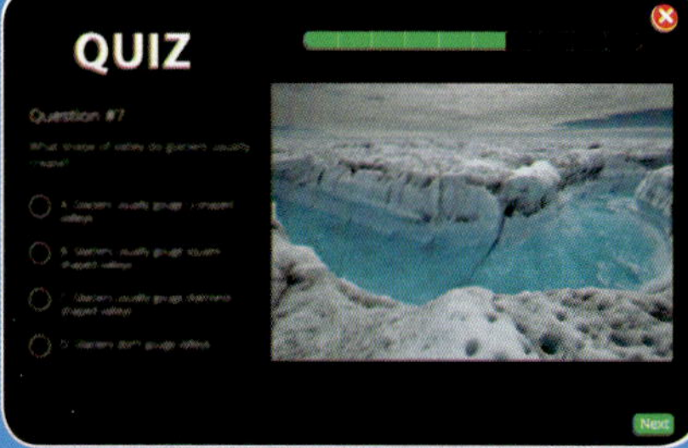

OPTIMIZED FOR

- ✓ TABLETS
- ✓ WHITEBOARDS
- ✓ COMPUTERS
- ✓ AND MUCH MORE!

Published by Smartbook Media Inc.
350 5th Avenue, 59th Floor New York, NY 10118
Website: www.openlightbox.com

Library of Congress Cataloging-in-Publication Data
Names: Gregory, Joy, author.
Title: Energy / Joy Gregory.
Other titles: American industries (Smartbook Media Inc.)
Description: New York, NY : Smartbook Media Inc., 2018. |
Series: American industries | Includes index.
Identifiers: LCCN 2016056288 (print) | LCCN 2016059888 (ebook) | ISBN 9781510519312 (hard cover : alk. paper) | ISBN 9781510519329 (multi-user ebk.)
Subjects: LCSH: Power resources--United States--Juvenile literature.
Classification: LCC TJ163.23 .G743 2018 (print) | LCC TJ163.23 (ebook) | DDC 333.790973--dc23
LC record available at https://lccn.loc.gov/2016056288

Printed in the United States of America in Brainerd, Minnesota
1 2 3 4 5 6 7 8 9 0 21 20 19 18 17

062017
032217

Editor: Katie Gillespie
Art Director: Terry Paulhus

Every reasonable effort has been made to trace ownership and to obtain permission to reprint copyright material. The publisher would be pleased to have any errors or omissions brought to its attention so that they may be corrected in subsequent printings. The publisher acknowledges Getty Images, iStock, Shutterstock, Dreamstime, Thinkstock, Alamy, and the United States Government Department of Energy as its primary image suppliers for this title.